MOUNTAINS
FOR
BREAKFAST

Geraldine Mitchell

MOUNTAINS
FOR
BREAKFAST

ARLEN
HOUSE

Mountains for Breakfast

is published in 2017 by
ARLEN HOUSE
42 Grange Abbey Road
Baldoyle, Dublin 13, Ireland
Phone: 00 353 86 8207617
arlenhouse@gmail.com
arlenhouse.blogspot.com

Distributed internationally by
SYRACUSE UNIVERSITY PRESS
621 Skytop Road, Suite 110
Syracuse, NY 13244–5290
Phone: 315–443–5534
Fax: 315–443–5545
supress@syr.edu
syracuseuniversitypress.syr.edu

ISBN 978–1–85132–164–3, paperback

cover image by Lisa Molina

CONTENTS

The poem is a code with no message:
The point of the mask is not the mask but the face underneath,
Absolute, incommunicado,
                                    unhoused and peregrine.

                                    – Charles Wright, 'Chickamauga'

MOUNTAINS
FOR
BREAKFAST

I

ABRACADABRA

This year, you say, you're taking up magic,
self-multiplication through sleight of mind,
the dislocation not of shoulder or hip

but of psyche,
a three-card trick
and each of you winning, each time.

This year, you say, you'll work at illusion,
at mirrors and smoke, the rabbit
and its hat, apparitions you alone need believe.

LANDFALL

i

Stop

Your name
on the locked
piano lid, your voice

quiet on the page. How long
since we spoke?
Bluebottles bounce

words from room to room,
old women's conversations
from the dead. The wind trawls

through lush montbretia,
stoppers the thrush's throat.

ii

Go

Wind tangles in rivers of air, catches
on trees, carries sheep bleat, dog bark
– lets them drop.

I am strung round with sounds
just out of meaning,
a chance to think

if I can hold off the prattle
of starlings, the scolding gulls.

iii

Pause

No speech. No sound.
My head hurts from
the silence.

Over the bay snow flings its
fraying upstrokes, grey on grey.
A bird's underside catches the sun,

angles its knife at my throat.

iv

Change

Scaldies toppled from their nest
by nature's bully bird, a gawky
changeling stranded in their place,

no more convincing than
Huck Finn in a frock – all wrists
and eyebrows, making hangdog look happy.

Poor plucked creature,
feathers gone, how
will you fly?

v

Stay

The islands are sucked dim this morning,
stirred pots of grey and green and
black: their turn for darkness.

Light colours our hill and the reeds
behind the shore: avocado and lime,
fresh-baked biscuit, a spill of gold –

and a *surge towards happiness* such as
Heaney said he felt, emerging into sunlight
from the *cold heart of the stone* of Gallarus.

ROADKILL

There's a hare on the road, its belly
soft as bilge, an eye already skewered,
crows impatient on the wire. I drag it

by the tip of one long slender ear to the
dignity of grass where birds will go on
feasting now breath has cooled

to air. Out west, the sky's a lesson
in geometry, radial trails of transatlantic
flights crisscross above Earth's camber

and all along the outstretched strand
knife-edged waves dice early morning shine
to foam, low rollers ramble in to die.

Before the light came on, before the STOP began to burn like the devil's eyes in that book we used to read to scare ourselves as children; before the intrusion into the dazzle of the afternoon of the beep-beep from somewhere hidden in the car, so alien we thought it was coming from the radio, that someone back in the studio, some relic of the eighties, still wore the sort of watch that beeped on the hour, the way people's phones go off now at plays and you purse your mouth in disgust until you realise it is your own mobile ringing from the bottom of your bag, underneath the coat and the umbrella and the packet of coffee bought at Spar on the way in, in case there isn't enough for morning; before the STOP lit up and glared steady as a devil, and the beep beeped, we had been sailing along the may-bedazzled road between Claremorris and Ballyhaunis as if we were immortal.

WHEN YOU PUT THE HEART ACROSS US ALL
for M.G.

The sky was an abstraction and the moon
peeled open her one blind eye on the huddle
of my back as news of your collapse
scratched from the mobile like a match-
boxed beetle. For a week the hills lay
comatose, cold bones and the thirst for light

in us all. We watched out for leaf burst, a kick-
start for April, chestnuts opening their fists, leaves
spilling like scarves from magicians' mouths
and the email, how it slid in one night
under the moon's closed lid with the news
that you had woken, were mended.

Nocturnal Visitors

I have come
to believe in ghosts,

those clothed shadows
that crowd the bed

like animals
whose nests have been disturbed.

They were at it again
last night,

bundled me into
a cartoon cat fight

round and round, fur
flying, me struggling

to keep a grip of myself,
not let them carry me off.

I told them to stop
and they did.

They mean no harm,
blind fingers skimming

the skin of my face,
mutely searching out

their place in memory,
wraiths come to find

an entry point,
a way into the light.

GHOST MOTH
Hepialus humuli

Its wings leave smudges on
the windowpane, thin dust rising
as it butts the glass, the moon
behind it and my lamp within.
I have been thinking too much

of my mother, gone these twenty years,
imagine she's come back to visit me.
What is it you want? Aren't you dead
long enough to leave me now,
to take your rest? I turn

the light out, watch the creature
crawl, pause, crawl – looking,
looking where to go next. I lie
and let it watch me too, wait
to see who's first to blink.

I think of her old coat
that smelled of comfort, dust and
Sundays – grey fur sleek as moonstone,
downy as the small grey hen
this morning at the market. I perch

restless on a varnished pew,
my cheek afloat on her sleeve,
listen for the sky's deep breath, hear
the hiccupping sea pour bucket-
fuls of water on the shore.

REMOTE CAPTURE

I'm caught in the shutter click
by the wrist, by the ankle,
I'm lying on a skim of gelatine

with my sisters and my cousins and we're
running through the stubble
soles like leather after six weeks

by the sea and we haven't seen our parents
since this morning and we're hungry
but don't know it, we're hopping

over rock pools, lifting seaweed,
bringing home a bucketful
of prawns. We're red and brown and

tousled, open-mouthed and laughing,
oh yes, we're laughing as we lurch
towards the camera's timeless eye.

I remember that day looking out the hotel window, a fishing boat half-submerged in the lake and small birds – ducks, coots, I don't remember anything as big as a swan – darting around and in the distance mountains and trees shivering in the February evening and how my eye was caught by something quite other, a small movement in the water which, for a moment, was that image in *Excalibur* when the sword comes up, a hand attached to it, and you can't help wondering what poor extra is down there, perished, holding her breath, waiting for the signal to surface and suddenly I am under water too, the ragged brown scar on the cold lake plunging me back into the canal at Killaloe when I fell in one wet August day and my parents kept on reading in their car, oblivious to the splash as my small body sank into the murk and with my eyes still open I plumbed down and down observing my descent until the movement was reversed and some phenomenon of buoyancy nudged me up again, light opened above my head, and I felt a rush of regret that my journey was over.

How the Body Remembers

Last night I was woken by a loose scrap of siren
and found you, face pressed to the night,
watching some drama unfold on our road,
cobalt strobing the silence

the way it lit up the street that September
in Trastevere, washed over you blue after blue
where you lay among fag ends and chair legs
until they lifted you on to a stretcher

and breath guttered back through your lungs
as we lunged over cobbles in a language
unknown to us and you found yourself
back in a nine-year-old body

careening through London's cacophony
of sirens, bomb flares through blue glass,
the City in flames, your eyes wide
with terror and me holding your hand.

HEATHER HONEY

The old house smelled of beeswax and
warm dust, the floors splintered; strange
people came and went, doors slammed
and women wept. *Grand-mère* raised
her voice and Pierre, her son, threw his
napkin in his plate and left. I clutched
my orange notebook marked 'Vocab.',
sensed something more than words – that

the honey scent of heather, hives humming
under shuttered windows all day long,
would not protect me from new grammar.
I learned to conjugate the tension between
adults, decline advances, parse glances
over coffee bowls at breakfast, note
whose eyes were red-rimmed, whose
honey-plastered *tartine* lay untouched.

WINTER COMMONS

Mountains for breakfast, the sea
for tea – there is no other food
to feast on. We eat winter's yellow
grass, its blackened branches, moss
that's fingers deep. We make soup of
stones, a solitary diet of grey rocks.

The hill has thrown a curtain of
snow across our window,
the trees that hem the garden
probe our sleep, scratch
the slated roof until
it squeals like chalk.

I dream of honeyed clover
on my tongue, the song of
the stream as it slips past
nettle, celandine, wild garlic.
I watch for the green mist
that soon must surely blur
the sycamore's stark nakedness.

NIGHT MUSIC

begins with
a breathy air
sketched through
gappy teeth
creeps closer in
three pairs of
squeaking shoes
swaps them
for a dozen
hobnailed boots
then come flung
fistfuls of loose
teeth spilled with
all their spittle
down the darkened
windowpanes
at five o'clock
dismembered furniture
is slung full force
against the house
splintered limbs
spark arcs of fire
by daybreak birdsong
crackles in smooth air.

II

DISCREDITED FORM, DISCREDITED SUBJECT MATTER
– after Charles Wright

01/01   Outside
nothing
beyond the veiled and misty hill.

02/01   Gulls fly slantwise
into raw wind.
                    Jackdaws.

Clare Island an inert shape
aslant, tipping
              down
                    to the east.

Wind.
An inexplicable clatter.

Sheep line the wall
for shelter.
Some gulls are high,
they ride the sky like buzzards.

03/01   The road runs with
braided water. I lie
thinking about verbs,
Annie Proulx, her
strong use of.

Rain, a heavy rope
paid out endlessly
from the sky.

Sudden sun flushes
Clare Island, low
cloud dapples
its flanks.

Sea
all lips
and nothing said.

04/01   Light infuses a grey sky,
an erasure
of darkness, of night, infinite
patience required to observe the

gradations, colour slowly
revealed. The sea –
hardly a colour at all, tinted

shine, a pastel sheen calling to mind
*the small desolations of forgotten lilies
and irises.*

09/01   Degrees of
wind, layered, insistent, rain
in fistfuls of grit.

Everybody's shouting but
which voice is loudest – the
Kalashnikov, the bombing
of a people?

Two lone gunmen ride
through the valley shooting,
shouting, and the noise
splits rocks, deafens us.

10/01   Wind, you threw your weight about again,
the windows let out little shrieks,
moisture came seeping through the wood.

                       O wind
it's past your bedtime, you've had your dance,
now lie down to sleep. Morning has begun

its furtive creep, the surf prepares a wide
white fringe for the beach. Thread yourself
through the trees' skinny bones, perch there
and rest.

11/01   This morning's
wind is still lumpish and loud.
Unfazed, five sheep graze
over the fence in R's field.

Black dash of a crow
across the window, white
splash of gull.

Your words spring from your landscape,
says Susan Howe.

12/01   Twenty past eight and day barely
here. Only the ghost of Clare Island
and yards of surf.

13/01   Drifts of hail.
                 Another raw day.

Not one wind, but many,
tongues of air lashing
the element they're made of.

14/01   I waited all night for the threatened storm.

Today *Charlie Hebdo* published
three million copies with the Prophet
on the cover. France really is
                          at war.

15/01   The house is coated with
salt and the winds still trumpet
through cracked cheeks.
It's said
          to get worse.
No sheep
(though it's hard to see
through salt-frosted panes).

They have found
shelter. The wind has
                     direction
but no destination.

17/01   I wake to a power cut.
Clare Island wrapped in a big wad
of wool, grubby and coming this way.

Porridge and coffee by candlelight.

Opalesque mountains, early sun on snow.

You begin to see better
how colours work off

each other – the layering,
the canvas showing through,
so you don't heed the picture so much
as the way it was painted,
the wonder of pigment and colour,
the glory of words on a page.

'You are not alone'
the poem said,
in the dark tunnel.

Out the window
I see a male pheasant, then a second,
running up R's field and through
the wire. Brief skirmish.
[Exit window left]

19/01   Monday.
           The silence of frost
           has paralysed the country,
           nothing moves –

When alone, on one of his distant assignments,
Kapuscinski would smoke in order to create a sense
of life, of company, something that moved. He
didn't want to smoke, but desperately needed some
sign of movement. Something like the terror of
silence when you have not even the notional
company of a clock, the tick-tock of time passing.

This is time stopped, lost time,
the silence of the bottom of the sea.

Silence = more than absence of sound
            = weight + absence of movement.

N's silence = absence = bell jar = dome
(see how quietly the snow falls) and
in L's painting of a fish
the mouth = silence.

21/01   The birds have begun to sing.
             The landscape is the same,
             withdrawn and bleached, but
             even the rain on the sky-
             light chirps.

22/01   Sun yesterday, sun today
             – a world transformed
             and possible.

23/01   I throw on a coat and run
             into the dawn to catch
             the signal from Y's call.
             My eye snags on a lone
             torch of flowering whin.
             The call drops.
             Listen.

             Shell to the ear,
             ear to the track,
             tracks in the sand,
             silver trickle of dry grain.

24/01   Woke sad –
                something unremembered.

Then I remember it, a long and complex dream where I was diagnosed with lung cancer and a woman was helping, she'd organise everything. But not yet. I had to wait. Then she told me she'd had to give an eye and they'd replaced it with the wrong colour. She showed me her blue eye.

25/01
Another dream. An angry man (my father?) shot the wall clock (white, round) with a pistol and it ran blood (black). He was angry about someone I protected. A bunch of letters were stuck in the letterbox. I shuffled through them. Nothing for me.

>What we know
>and don't say
>is huge as
>imagination
>
>a parallel
>world
>where we keep
>memories
>
>three bags full –
>one buried, one
>split and leaking
>feathers

28/01   Gobstopper
                words roll
                under the couch

dust balls
they lie there
in the vault

29/01   stomach-sick
panic of mouse
round and round she goes nosing
the sides and corners of a cage
with a roof, a floor, walls
but no door

31/01   a feeling of something
ending, the way the heart
can sometimes sink
at the turn for home

rain pats the window
with a kitten's paw

[January 2015]

III

CEPHALALGIA

I am obsessed with all things cerebral,
that is to say, anything
resembling a brain – reeled

into folds, folded into crevices,
I dream of ruched camisoles,
winding cloths, swaddles and shrouds.

I have developed a kitten's weakness for wool,
balls that unspool into labyrinths,
an attraction to circuit boards,

tangles of fishing line, coiled snakes and
smoke rings, worm casts at
low tide, cephalopod molluscs, the cochlea

in each of my cat's ears
– all because
the walnut lodged in my skull

will not surrender the ink-soaked
husk that hugs the grooved shell
that shelters the membrane that papers

the twin hemispheres
that make up the soft part,
the sore heart of my head.

SNEAK

Age comes, and then
infirmity, not beating
on the door with knotty

stick, announcing its
arrival with due pomp
and medication, but

insinuating noxious
vapours into lung and heart,
round knee and hip, curling

through the brain like smoke,
invisible yet choking with
an acrid autumn smell.

NAMED

The sea was tame that afternoon,
the hills radiant and clear.
Once the word was out it hung
between us, drifted
into boots and shoes, half-opened drawers.

Inflated by our silence it hardened
into menace, squeezed up against
the ceiling, pressed us back
against the walls, forced its way
underneath the chair you'd just sat down on.

The word was out, a monster now
in Tyrolean hat. I opened the front door,
walked out on both of you.

An orange sun floated
into the baffled sea.
I watched it go. *Tell it,*
tell it, a curlew cried.
Alzheimer's, I replied.

SWARM

Bees from a hive, words
brim your parted lips,

spill in brindled columns,
crawl my skin, envelop me

gently,
gently sting.

CONUNDRUM

Spring and a dying mind,
what am I to make of that?

Wait for the sun to burn off
the mist, for the first big rains

to flush the ditches. Trust
the hares will be back,

their white-trimmed ears
attentive and forgiving.

The hens are busy all day long,
the sheep pursue a logic

of their own, the dogs
another, and I am lost

for words and you
have lost your words

and I cannot step inside your head
to help you find them.

WHO KILLED COCK ROBIN, WHEN DID HE DIE

I pick it limp
by its prickle feet,
lay it in my palm,

watch the feathers
of its rusted breast,
try to figure out

the space between living
and death, the race
between breath and air,

rake the leaves
around the wind-bent
ash, hold fistfuls to

my face, try to
catch the beat of
the old tree's pulse.

WHAT THE THREAT OF THUNDER DOES

when dry wind lashes
tall trees and sounds
plash in small bushes

and sparrows stab the afternoon
in the hollow of its back
and from the next village

a circular saw ratchets
the air to an edge and
temperatures thicken

clouds roll from all sides
mountains never so close
until now and

the afternoon grumbles
to a halt finds its
dead hour sky low

swifts slit paunched air
till it shrieks and the rumble
spreads, it is close now

there are shouts and suddenly
hooves on packed earth and
the thunder is here it's right here

in a frenzy of dust it
explodes through
the loafing afternoon.

Walk out –
talk back to hedges
hidden birds

the blind woman
on her chair by the door
talk to the dead

the too many lost
and the drowned
– far as you go

you will always come back
empty-handed
to the here and the now

bird song and leaf sway
the plane tree's marled trunk
corporeal and dense

and rooted as ever.

AFTER RAIN

It is not enough
            sometimes
      after rain
to watch the sun
 find surfaces
     to shine on –
 thin wires lit,
fine threads
 that bind wet fields,
    stitch hedge to hedge
with streaks of silver –
              some days
we have no heart for play
when the sun comes calling
    with rainbows
thick enough to skip with.

All I see is the entrance to the burrow of your skull: two dark moons defined by absence, desolate as rock pools brimming on the ebb tide of blind night. Outside the world is loud, is bright, is brash, is busy, is the crash of cymbals. You curtain your eyes with the fan of your uncertain hand.

The night has blown drifts over the rest of your face, sand fills your mouth and marram grass catches in the silt of grains. The topography of dunes shifts constantly. You wake to a new geography, abandon the old map, peer at the compass you have owned for years, strange now, unfamiliar as a toy rashly ordered on the internet.

The burrow holes are dark and filled with absence. This morning a full moon drifted down the smooth October sky – an ocular globe slipped of its orbit to float to America, as fixed on its course as the needle of the compass you hold.

From inside your dark hide what did you see? What comfort in that round, white, mottled face?

THRESHOLD

Day breaks, light bleeds, and I imagine
blackbirds on the grass back home
listening with their feet; our robin,

not yet ripe for singing, peeved by
the skill of finches spearing nuts;
a gang of sparrows cheerful underneath

the rhododendron's damp-dark leaves.
My eye is caught by rooks around
the litter bins, portly and severe

as undertakers, already single-mindedly
intent on their predations. I consider
the immortality of birds, the unexamined

reassurance of their scavenging, as if
they were the same ones year on year.
A breeze blows up, the window

keens, its red blind slaps the grey glass.
Beside your bed oxygen bubbles,
your breath is like wind in a hedge.

LOCUS

An agitated day, the wind
not knowing which way to blow,
clouds stacked in tattered ranks.

Low sun breaks through, the hill
for a moment lit, scars and raised welts,
old bones exposed.

RAPPEL

As if you had swallowed a mouse
from an illustrated manuscript,
a bootlace smile suggests itself

on your still face, the tail lain
sleek across your lips. Palestrina
is on repeat and the nurses have

set up a makeshift altar in the corner
of the room, the crucifix turned
to the wall, a spray of fake

sweet pea, bottle of holy water.
We sit with your still-warm body,
your bare arms cooling slow

as stone on a summer night.
But it is November and dark,
I will coil this morning's rope,

pay it out, pull it in again
until my hands chafe, my eyes
smart in the chill salt wind.

If we had a keen vision and feeling of all human life, it would be like hearing the grass grow and the squirrel's heartbeat, and we should die of that roar which lies on the other side of silence.
— George Eliot, *Middlemarch*

I listen beyond the grave into the ground, the air, through layers of clay and ether where language is neither alphabet nor words, yet speaks, like a figure buried under snow.

When we buried you, three months before, it was easy digging the still-soft ground. Now my spade hits as I start to lift the icy crystals, pile by pile. I expect nothing. Then I see you, looking up, your face not smiling, not angry either, your hair amiss (but then it always was).

Speak to me and I will listen – or should that be: *If I listen, will you speak?* Or do I simply imagine it all: *hearing the grass grow and the squirrel's heartbeat*, snow in the black January night.

IV

Heart of Stone

i

A stone has lodged
next my heart, cold,
hard against the

throb, now pump,
now ruffled bird.
It's a child's game:

paper, scissors,
stone. It's Russian
roulette. Stubbed

impulse of affection.
Concussed love.
Sometimes blood

sisters – stone stands up
for heart, heart pleads for
stone, bleeds rubies.

ii

Stone is lonely where it lies,
its eyes are dull, its thoughts
sealed in, sensation all outside
– the feel of soles, heels
endless on its unforgiving shell.

Stone dreams, feels fear, stone's mind
runs down streams and gullies, gathers
into uproar.

Stone tumbles
in sea's arms, recalls the pulse
of salmon's belly tick-ticking on
its own thick skin.

Stone cannot move, but atoms swizzle,
dance their own particular dance (that much
it knows).

iii

Stone lies in the riverbed,
on a cushion of mud,
in the comfort of muffled sound.

It feels the thrill of
water rushing head
long over it.

Which is better? The rush to
the ocean, its mix and abandon,
or here, nursing the purpose of time?

iv

This morning stone feels light
     as polyester, brittle
     as a film set boulder in a Western.
All night the water lay still, dark
     as a tunnel, quiet
     as a Monday morning mosque.
Today its skin feels thin
     as a skim of new ice, thin
     as the skin around your heart
the day the dogs' muzzles are off, their barks sharp
     as teeth, their eyes mean.
Its heart in its mouth is
     like a stone in theirs,
     the clatter, the foam
     and slide of saliva,
          the pink tongue.

WANTING

A trail of mottled feathers
behind the blue hydrangea,
the headless body
of a thrush.

All that remains
when the merlin
has emptied the garden
of song.

EBB

i

Days pay out
thin as string

light frays
through mesh

even the rain is a veil
no body, no weight

some days
words shrivel

curl
like burnt paper

stop up my mouth
like ash

ii

                I rattle
from room to room
                a shrunken Alice

one arm
        sheared off at the
                shoulder and the house

an empty bag
        turned inside out

a room
        I cannot find
                a door

AFTER THE FUNERAL

The house is raucous with ghosts:
four generations jostle from boxes,
elbow each other out of envelopes,
squirm from plastic pouches
to frolic in the silence of the dark.

They eye each other up, smile
at svelter selves, the youthful
innocence, regret the time it took
for wisdom to appear. By dawn
they have resumed their old

positions: the young boy holds
his mother's hand, she smiles,
he gestures towards the sunset with
his walking stick, she is once more
demure and bonneted and six.

LOST NEGATIVE

In the lost negative
you exist
– Robert Lowell, 'For Sheridan'

Which is as much as to say
you are a pale-lipped ghost now,
white tie and lapels, buttons
snowmanning the abysmal

slope, chased by a cat under
leaves, disappearing
between the pages of an album,
or, who knows, surfacing

in an Appalachian village where
a woman stirs a mixture, tongs
a slip of paper, flips it over
till it's done, hangs it on a line

like laundry. Turns you around.
I walk that village every day
at dawn when the birds come
tapping with their beaks of horn.

COUNSEL

I stand under a blanket
of blind stars, the night cool
as a desert corridor.

The kitchen
throws a knife of light
along the gravel at my feet.

SEA GARDEN

I'll go no further
than the low stone
wall, its rusted gate

leaning like a soldier
on a crutch. The wind
has dropped, sky's mouth

clapped shut, clothes
hang easy from the line.
This garden's space

enough to stage small
miracles: if I sit still
I'll see plants grow, hear

cells divide, stems
thicken and unfold
until earth's crust cracks,

leaves break through,
like seals' heads
surfacing to sun.

FIFTH OF JULY
after Tomas Tranströmer's 'Golden Wasp'

Today is the fifth of July, the sky
painterly with broken cloud,
the sea a layered sheen – blue, grey,
milky green. Fescue, nettles and
young alders sway in pliant
ranks, the smallest to the front.

Today is the fifth of July, starlings
scourge the sycamore with sharpening
jabber, jolt it to its roots;
down the road jackdaws are busy
swagging the phone lines
with black bows.

I toss a coin, land it in a rock-
pool, watch it zig and zag, undo
the sand, set the green weed swaying.
Fish flicker from all sides, *what now,*
they mouth, *what now, what now.*

St John's Eve, Maam Valley

It's half past ten, the place
between dog and wolf
where light
       oh-so-politely
retires
with only the faintest
click of the latch.

Some clouds at the back
are hugging themselves,
holding on to the memory of sun,

calling the eye on,
come on,
what are ye afraid of?

WOMAN ALONE

When I wake

darkness

five strokes
of a church bell
close-by   the room
conceals its contours,
the narrow bed its thin quilt.

The brick floor grits underfoot
like blown sand
as I move to the window,
push open shutters on air
smooth with the promise of heat.

The wake of the ringing
washes the walls of the cobbled street
and above furrowed rooftops
                    stars
waver like sparks,
lustre the air with lost notes.

I lean on the sill, feel
the mystery of sound emerging
from silence, returning into it, of being
in time, then out of it,
                    the thinning night,
how my day has been changed before it's begun
and no-one to know it but me.

GRIEF

    stumbles
in black gloves
      down unlit cul-de-sacs
where words silt up in drifts –
                spilt tesserae,
    redundant letters
that can no longer find their way
        or seek each other out to spell
    how did it come to this?

    Grief wavers
on the indrawn breath
of a day not yet begun,
        in a shroud of mist unsettled
by the rummage of birds;

    breaks
on the grace note
      of a wren.

THE LIGHT WITHIN US
from a line by Brian Turner

is light through a keyhole, a curtain
crack in an upstairs window. It's
glow worms in Brittany, yellow
tulips, children's laughter from the
river, an old man's lined face by
candlelight, or a poem by Rumi, or a
look, or a smile, or a word, like hope.

SEA CHANGE

I have come to a place where the sea
opens and closes small fists in a dance.

A place of remembering, replacing
the centre of gravity, restoring

sap where it can rise again,
where thin air finds gaps enough

to sing through. I have been
relocated to silence, my body

no longer incorrigible, a voice
spooling in my throat that surely

cannot be mine. This is a place
of revision, I will have time to name

the changing colours of the sea. I'll
wait beside the ocean, search slim

bands of foam, dishevelled froth, find
a hoard of sea glass, misted gifts.

SOMETIMES MAGIC HAPPENS

A glister of swans
against a gunmetal sky,

a ruffle of crows
on a fence, sun

pouring incandescence
over an indifferent sea.

Deer leap into the road
just as it says on the sign

and a bus driver juggles apples
as he waits for the lights to change.

P. 33

The title of the sequence is a line from Charles Wright's 'Apologia Pro Vita Sua' (*Black Zodiac*, Farrar, Straus, and Giroux, 1997)

> Journal and landscape
> —Discredited form, discredited subject matter—

P. 34

'... the small desolations of forgotten lilies and irises', comes from Marilynne Robinson's *Housekeeping* (Farrar, Straus, and Giroux, 1980)

P. 35

'Your words spring from your landscape', is from an interview with Susan Howe, 'Detective Work', published on the Poetry Foundation's website in January 2015 (https://www.poetryfoundation.org/features/articles/detail/70 196)

P. 37

'You are not alone'
the poem said,
in the dark tunnel.

From 'October' by Louise Glück, in her collection *Averno* (Farrar, Straus, and Giroux, 2006)

Acknowledgements

Acknowledgements are due to the editors of the following publications: *Poetry Ireland Review, Poetry London, Southword, The Interpreter's House, The Irish Times, The Rialto.*

'Ghost Moth' appears in *Washing Windows? Irish Women Write Poetry* edited by Alan Hayes (Arlen House, 2017)

'Grief' appears in *Fermata – Writings Inspired by Music* edited by Eva Bourke and Vincent Woods (Artisan House, 2016)

'How the Body Remembers' was placed third in the 2014 Strokestown International Poetry Competition

An earlier version of 'Cephalalgia' was shortlisted for The Plough Prize in 2014

I am deeply grateful to the following people for their generous support: Moya Cannon, Aoife Casby, Mags Duffy, Kathleen Jamie, Michael Longley, Alice Lyons, John Murphy and Jean Tuomey.

Once again, my thanks to Alan Hayes of Arlen House.

About the Author

Geraldine Mitchell is the author of *World Without Maps* (2011) and *Of Birds and Bones* (2014), both published by Arlen House. She has also written a biography of Muriel Gahan, *Deeds Not Words* (Town House, 1997) and two novels for young people, *Welcoming the French* (1992) and *Escape to the West* (1994), published by Attic Press.

In 2008 Geraldine won the Patrick Kavanagh Poetry Award. That year she was also awarded a Mayo County Council Bursary to the Tyrone Guthrie Centre and, in 2011, a literature bursary from the Arts Council/An Chomhairle Ealaíon. Other awards include the Amergin Prize for poetry and the inaugural Trócaire-Poetry Ireland Poetry Prize. She has twice been shortlisted for the Strokestown International Poetry Prize, coming third in 2014.

Born in Dublin, Geraldine has been living on the Co. Mayo coast since 2000. She has a degree in English and French from Trinity College, Dublin and a Masters in English Literature from the University of Aix-en-Provence. She lived in France, Algeria, Spain and England, teaching English and working as a freelance journalist, before returning to Ireland in 1992.

Geraldine acted as Poetry Ambassador for Trócaire from 2012 to 2015 and is part of the Writers in Schools programme run by Poetry Ireland.

www.geraldinemitchell.net